ECONOMY IN ACTION!

LABOR & MANAGEMENT

Megan M. Gunderson
ABDO Publishing Company

visit us at
www.abdopublishing.com

Published by ABDO Publishing Company, PO Box 398166, Minneapolis, MN 55439. Copyright © 2013 by Abdo Consulting Group, Inc. International copyrights reserved in all countries. No part of this book may be reproduced in any form without written permission from the publisher. The Checkerboard Library™ is a trademark and logo of ABDO Publishing Company.

Printed in the United States of America, North Mankato, Minnesota.
052012
092012

 PRINTED ON RECYCLED PAPER

Cover Photo: Alamy
Interior Photos: Alamy p. 26; AP Images pp. 17, 25; Corbis p. 5; Getty Images pp. 15, 16, 19, 21, 23; iStockphoto pp. 1, 11; Neil Klinepier p. 13; Photo Researchers p. 7; Thinkstock p. 9; US National Archives and Records Administration p. 22

Editors: Tamara L. Britton, BreAnn Rumsch
Art Direction: Neil Klinepier

Library of Congress Cataloging-in-Publication Data

Gunderson, Megan M., 1981-
 Labor & management / Megan M. Gunderson.
    p. cm. -- (Economy in action!)
 Includes index.
 ISBN 978-1-61783-488-2
 1. Economics--Juvenile literature. 2. Labor unions--Juvenile literature. I. Title. II. Title: Labor and management.
 HA29.6.G86 2013
 338--dc23
                        2012014364

Contents

Your Economy

Have you heard words like *labor* and *management*? Do you think they have anything to do with you? They do! They're related to business. Business is a key part of the economy. And you're an important part of the economy, too.

Chances are, you've spent money at some time in your life. Maybe you spend money at the movies every week. Or maybe you remember saving up to buy something special.

Where did the money you spent come from? Did you labor long hours babysitting? Did someone give you birthday money?

When you spent your money, you became part of the nation's economy. You may not be the head of a major company. But you're still an important part of how business works. Keep reading to find out how labor and management relate to you and everyone you know.

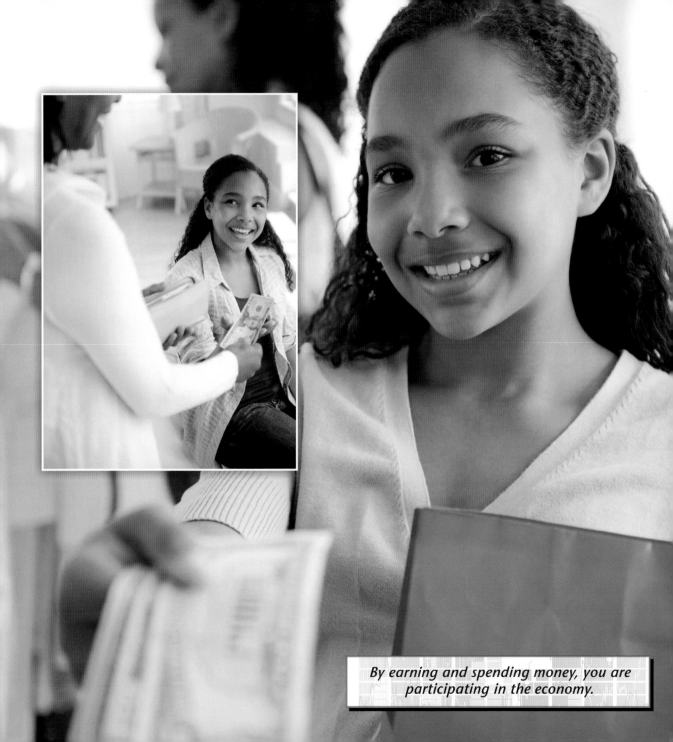

By earning and spending money, you are participating in the economy.

What Is a Business?

Labor and management are two key elements of any business. So what is a business? The simplest answer is that a business provides goods or services.

What are goods and services? Goods are things you can get your hands on. That includes everything from video games to washing machines.

Services are something you experience. You're using services every time you visit the dentist or have your recycling picked up.

Businesses are a key part of today's economy. In order to produce goods and provide services, they hire labor. If you are employed, you're part of the labor force. And, you're making money.

With money, you can buy the things you need and want. Ideally, you have money for food, housing, and clothing with some left over. When you spend some of the money you've earned, you support businesses.

People work together to get things done because it's more efficient than working alone.

Who is in charge of businesses? Management! These are the people who hire laborers. They also decide what and how much to produce. Their decisions help keep people employed. These people with jobs then have money to spend. It's all one big circle!

Entrepreneurs

Why do people start businesses? One **incentive** is to make a profit. Another is simply to provide a needed good or service.

These incentives can lead to **innovation**. People come up with new or improved products. Then they're offering something no one else can provide! This can help a business be successful.

Yet not all businesses succeed. So, the people who start them must be willing to take that risk. But if everything goes well, they make money.

Are you an entrepreneur? That's a big word! It simply means you have a great idea. And, you decide to take the risk of starting a business.

Let's say you realize a lot of people in your neighborhood need help mowing their lawns. You have a riding lawn mower, free time, and the need to make money. So, you decide to start a lawn mowing business. That makes you the management.

FUN FACT

There are more than 30 million businesses in the United States.

To get started, you'll need **capital**, labor, and **natural resources**. Capital includes your supplies, such as a lawn mower and the gas to run it.

If your business grows, you won't be able to do everything yourself. You'll need to hire extra labor. Your business will also depend on natural resources such as water and the sun. These help grass grow.

In the United States and Canada, people are able to start businesses because the economy is based on a free market. This means business managers, not governments, decide what to produce and how much to sell it for.

Making a Profit

How will your business make a profit? Part of managing your business is deciding how much to charge people for your service. The amount should cover your expenses and leave you with money left over. The money left over is your profit.

For a lawn mowing business, you would have to consider your operating costs. These include equipment repairs and gas. You'll also have to decide how much to pay the people you hire for their labor.

If you charge customers too little, you won't make enough to pay for all these things. What if you charge too much or provide low quality? People may decide they don't need the service you are offering.

The economy also affects whether people use your service. When it is in trouble, people may make less money. They may even lose their jobs. In that case, they won't be able to pay someone to mow their lawns.

That's how a suffering economy can affect even the smallest businesses. During the **Great Recession**, many people lost their jobs. They earned less money. So, they had less to spend on other businesses.

Competition is an important part of running a business. Try providing better service than another lawn company at the same price. This could help you gain customers.

Supply & Demand

Now you know that businesses must consider **capital** and labor. Several other things also affect their success.

Imagine a chocolate candy bar business. How much of the product should be made? And how much will people have to pay to buy it? Economic forces called supply and demand determine the answers to these questions.

Supply is the amount of a product the producers are willing and able to make and sell for a certain price. Is the price high? Then managers will want to make more chocolate bars. They'll make lots of money selling them! Is the price low? Then they won't want to make as many.

Demand is the amount of a product the consumers are willing and able to buy for a certain price. If your chocolate bars cost a lot, people won't buy as many. If they don't cost much, people will be able to buy more.

Ideally, you should make the same amount of chocolate bars as people are willing to buy. When the price is right, supply equals demand. When that happens, it's called the equilibrium price.

Prices naturally work their way toward equilibrium. What if the chocolate bars cost a lot? There will be more supply than consumers are willing to buy. This is called a **surplus**. It will cause the price to drop.

If the price drops too low, people will demand more bars than have been supplied. The bars will be **scarce**. That will make the price to buy them rise again.

Inflation

Do the adults in your life ever say things like, "I remember when movies cost a dollar"? A movie ticket did used to cost less. The reason for that is inflation.

Put simply, inflation means prices are going up and the value of money is going down. A movie ticket that cost $8.00 ten years ago might cost $10.50 now. You have to spend more of your money to get the same product! That means the buying power of your money has gone down.

There's another way to look at how inflation affects your money. The same amount of money won't buy you as much anymore. In the past, maybe $5.00 could buy you a large bag of popcorn. But now, it only gets you a medium.

Still, this isn't all bad. What if people borrowed money to start a business? Now, they're paying their **debts** with less valuable money. That's good for them.

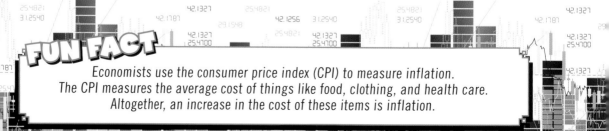

FUN FACT

Economists use the consumer price index (CPI) to measure inflation. The CPI measures the average cost of things like food, clothing, and health care. Altogether, an increase in the cost of these items is inflation.

How many hours did you have to babysit to make enough money for your movie ticket? If prices rise, will you charge more for your services next time?

However, it's bad for the people who lent the money. The money the lenders are getting back is worth less than the money lent out.

Inflation is also bad for people who save money. They have the same dollar amount in the bank. But it won't buy them as much as before.

Governments try hard to make sure inflation doesn't get out of control. There are two main types. The hard part is knowing which kind is happening.

Demand-pull inflation is one type. It happens when the demand for goods and services is more than the supply. Costs go up because there's more money than there are goods to buy.

Governments can control this type with taxes. If people pay higher taxes, they have less money to spend.

Governments can also stop buying as many goods. That means businesses don't sell as much. So, they pay their workers less. This makes people spend less, which reduces demand.

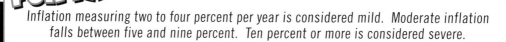

FUN FACT

Inflation measuring two to four percent per year is considered mild. Moderate inflation falls between five and nine percent. Ten percent or more is considered severe.

A two percent inflation rate is considered ideal for economic growth.

Cost-push inflation is another type. When the price of making goods goes up, businesses must charge more for their products. If prices go up, workers need to make more money. That way, they can still buy things.

What if businesses can't afford to pay their workers more? People may lose their jobs. With more people out of work, less money is being spent. Once again, this slows inflation.

Deflation Dangers

Too much inflation can be dangerous. So the opposite must be better, right? Wrong! Deflation is not healthy, either.

When deflation happens, prices go down. And, the value of money goes up. So, you can buy more goods and services with less money. But that means businesses will make less.

Let's say there's a fancy toy you want to buy. Today, it costs $100. If deflation is occurring, that toy might only cost $90 in a few months. So, you decide to wait until the price drops. Why spend more now when you can get it for less later?

If everyone waits to make purchases, businesses suffer. They stop making and selling as many products. If they cut labor costs to save money, there are more people out of work.

How do governments fight against deflation? Governments can print more money. And, they can lower **interest** rates. This makes people more likely to borrow money.

HYPERINFLATION

Hyperinflation has happened several memorable times. Germany had huge debts to pay after World War I. So, the government just printed lots of extra money. That way, they had plenty to pay back what they owed. But this had terrible results!

German money quickly lost its value. In 1919, 1 US dollar was worth a little more than 8 German marks. By 1923, a dollar could buy more than 4 trillion marks! Money was so worthless people used it as fuel, wallpaper, and even toys.

Zimbabwe faced a similar problem in the 2000s. At one point, its monthly inflation rate reached 76 billion percent! Banks even printed bills worth 100 trillion Zimbabwean dollars. Eventually, the only solution was to completely abandon the currency.

Unemployment

When economic growth is less than perfect, businesses sometimes cut costs by cutting labor. Then you might hear a lot of news about unemployment.

If someone is unemployed, he or she doesn't have a job. Yet the term doesn't apply to absolutely everyone who isn't working. It only refers to people who are able to work and are actively seeking jobs. They are considered part of the labor force.

Some people without jobs are not considered unemployed. They might be students or stay-at-home parents. They could also be retired, ill, or not seeking work for other reasons.

People become unemployed in several ways. Some are fired from their jobs. Others are laid off when a company must cut costs or close. A few workers may also choose to leave their jobs before finding new ones.

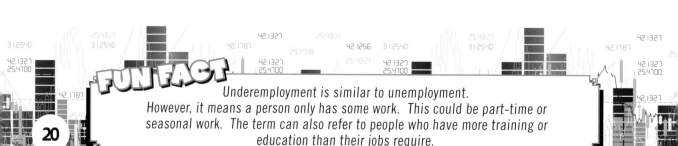

FUN FACT

Underemployment is similar to unemployment. However, it means a person only has some work. This could be part-time or seasonal work. The term can also refer to people who have more training or education than their jobs require.

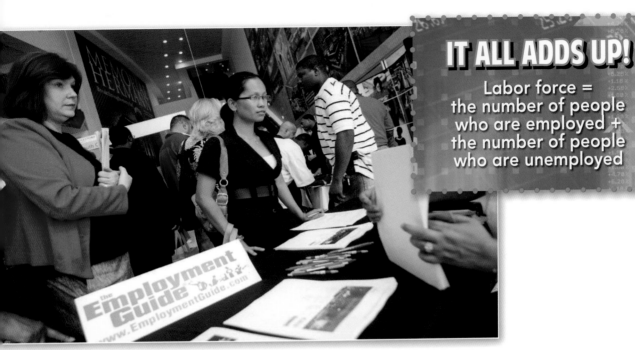

In 2011, nearly 14 million people in the United States were unemployed. The unemployment rate for the year was 8.9%.

The unemployment rate is a measure of how much of the labor force is out of work. In the United States, the Department of Labor's Bureau of Labor Statistics reports on this rate. It is one way to measure how healthy the economy is.

For most governments, the goal is full employment. That doesn't mean every single person in the country has a job. There are always some people who are between jobs for a short time. But, governments want the unemployment rate to be as close to zero percent as possible.

Is your mom facing unemployment? What about your friend's dad? This can be very hard on a family. If people can't find new jobs, they have to rely on their savings. Once savings run out, people may have trouble paying their bills.

Luckily, there are programs to help. The United States and Canada both offer unemployment insurance (UI). In the United States, UI was established by the Social Security Act of 1935.

UI is not a long-term solution. Rather, it is meant to assist people during the time it takes them to find a new job. This is helpful if they want to remain part of the labor force.

In the United States, each state has its own system of UI. Workers must meet certain requirements to qualify for the program.

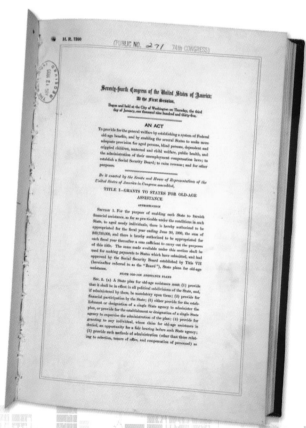

The Social Security Act

Is your mom willing and able to work? Is your friend's dad actively trying to find work? Then they may qualify to get a weekly paycheck for a while. This will help them pay for food and their homes until they find new jobs.

UI is helpful for individuals as well as businesses. Since they're still receiving some income, people can continue to purchase goods and services. This helps keep the economy going.

President Franklin D. Roosevelt signing the Social Security Act

COBRA

In the United States, losing a job can also mean losing health insurance. Luckily, many people qualify for a program called COBRA. This allows people to pay to keep the group health insurance offered by their employer. This can be costly. But for many people, it is less expensive than paying for their own plans.

Labor Unions

Management makes decisions about how a business is run. When a business is doing poorly, management may decide to cut labor to save money. Like UI, labor unions are a way people get help after job loss. They represent the interests of a business's labor force.

Labor unions usually represent a group of people who all work in the same trade or type of job. One common type of union is for automobile workers. Chances are, your teachers are also part of a union. Even NBA players can join a union.

Members usually pay **dues** to be a part of a union. In return, the union takes care of its members. It helps unemployed members find new jobs. It also tries to guarantee fair working conditions, hours, and hiring and firing practices. A union also organizes strikes.

FUN FACT

Labor Day is celebrated on the first Monday of September in the United States. Sometimes, labor organizations host events on this day that honors workers.

During a strike, a union may use dues to help pay members while they are out of work.

Employees may go on strike to get a business to meet their demands. They might want better health care or higher wages. They may want a business to cut costs in ways other than cutting labor. Until these demands are met, employees stop working. This harms the business.

How do unions reach their goals? One major way is through collective bargaining. This is when union officials representing workers **negotiate** with a business's management.

Why do unions use collective bargaining? It gives them more power in the situation.

Think of it this way. Have you ever tried to convince your teacher to give you an extra day to finish your homework? You might have been more successful if the whole class had worked together. Asking as a group can give you a better chance of getting what you want.

People have the right to be in a union and bargain collectively because of the National Labor Relations Act of 1935. There are obvious benefits to being part of a union. Members earn more than nonmembers. They are also more likely to have health care.

However, not everyone believes unions should be allowed. **Corruption** has been an issue in the past. A union may get very large. And, it may seem to have too much power over how management runs a business.

A healthy relationship between labor and management is a key part of a successful economy. When businesses run well, they can hire more labor. And when people are employed, they earn money they can use to fuel the economy. This cycle keeps the economy growing!

COLLECTIVE BARGAINING LAWS

In 2011, Wisconsin tried to cut spending by limiting collective bargaining by government employees. Many people protested. However, the governor felt this was necessary during difficult economic times.

Other states passed similar laws. State workers in New York agreed not to get raises for two years. And an Ohio law eliminated most collective bargaining for police officers and firefighters. But, voters later overturned this decision.

MAJOR LABOR ORGANIZATIONS

Can you match the labor organization with the types of workers it represents?

1. American Federation of State, County and Municipal Employees (AFSCME)

2. American Federation of Labor and Congress of Industrial Organizations (AFL-CIO)

3. Teamsters Union

4. United Automobile, Aerospace and Agricultural Implement Workers of America (UAW)

a) public employees and health care workers

b) truck drivers, food-processing plant workers, automobile salespeople, and others

c) auto parts workers, higher education workers, gaming workers, and others

d) building and construction, maritime, transportation, and other unions

Answer Key: 1.a 2.d 3.b 4.c

GOODS & SERVICES

Which are goods and which are services?

dentist

bicycle repair

books

iPod

haircut

city bus

doctor

swimming lessons

bicycle

shoes

video games

How many goods and services do you use in a week? Keep track and make a list!

THE DOLLAR OVER TIME

Inflation and deflation affect how much your money is worth. Imagine you bought goods and services for $100 in 1920. How much would you need to spend to buy the same products in different years?

1920	$100	1970	$193.81
1930	$83.33	1980	$411.08
1940	$69.91	1990	$652.00
1950	$120.06	2000	$859.23
1960	$147.65	2010	$1159.68

Glossary

capital - the factories and equipment owned by a business and used to make money.

corruption - dishonesty or improper behavior.

debt (DEHT) - something owed to someone, especially money.

dues - a charge or a fee, such as for membership.

Great Recession - beginning in 2007, a period of time when business activity slowed.

incentive - something that urges someone to do something.

innovation - a new idea, method, or device.

interest - money paid for the use or borrowing of money.

natural resource - a material found in nature that is useful or necessary to life. Water, forests, and minerals are examples of natural resources.

negotiate (nih-GOH-shee-ayt) - to work out an agreement about the terms of something.

scarce (SKEHRS) - an amount less than what is needed.

surplus - an amount above what is needed.

Web Sites

To learn more about the economy in action, visit ABDO Publishing Company online. Web sites about labor and management are featured on our Book Links page. These links are routinely monitored and updated to provide the most current information available.

www.abdopublishing.com

Index